A Guide to Study Skills

A Guide to Study Skills

Revised Edition

Meera Ravi

Viva Books

New Delhi | Mumbai | Chennai | Kolkata | Bangalore | Hyderabad | Kochi | Guwahati

First Published 2005
Revised Edition 2007, Reprinted 2010

VIVA BOOKS PRIVATE LIMITED

- 4737/23 Ansari Road, Daryaganj, New Delhi 110 002
  E-mail: vivadelhi@vivagroupindia.net, Tel. 42242200
- 76, Service Industries, Shirvane, Sector 1, Nerul, Navi Mumbai 400 706
  E-mail: vivamumbai@vivagroupindia.net, Tel. 27721273, 27721274
- Jamals Fazal Chambers, 26 Greams Road, Chennai 600 006
  E-mail: vivachennai@vivagroupindia.net, Tel. 28290304, 28294241
- B-103, Jindal Towers, 21/1A/3 Darga Road, Kolkata 700 017
  E-mail: vivakolkata@vivagroupindia.net, Tel. 22836381, 22816713
- 7, Sovereign Park Apartments, 56-58, K. R. Road, Basavanagudi, Bangalore 560 004
  E-mail: vivabangalore@vivagroupindia.net, Tel. 26607409, 26607410
- 101-102 Mughal Marc Aptt., 3-4-637 to 641, Narayanguda, Hyderabad 500 029
  E-mail: vivahyderabad@vivagroupindia.net, Tel. 27564481, 27564482
- First Floor, Beevi Towers, SRM Road, Kaloor, Kochi 682 018, Kerala
  E-mail: vivakochi@vivagroupindia.net, Tel: 0484-2403055, 2403056
- 232, GNB Road, Beside UCO Bank, Silpukhuri, Guwahati 781 003
  E-mail: vivaguwahati@vivagroupindia.net, Tel: 0361-2666386

www.vivagroupindia.com

ISBN 978-81-309-0828-1

Published by Vinod Vasishtha for Viva Books Private Limited, 4737/23, Ansari Road, Daryaganj, New Delhi - 110 002. Printed and bound by Raj Press, R-3, Inderpuri, New Delhi - 110 012.

CONTENTS

Preface *vii*
A Special Word for Children *ix*

1. Knowing Yourself 01
2. Attitude 02
3. Having Positive Attitude When Things Go Wrong 05
4. Why Study? 08
5. Introduction to Study Techniques 10
6. Case Study 11
7. Anxiety Quiz 14
8. General Tips 15
9. Concentration 17
10. Emotional Disturbance 25
11. Memory Tips 28
12. The Power of 'Attention' 30
13. Some Introspection 33
14. Why Procrastinate? 35
15. Willpower 37
16. Group Study – Some Guidelines 41
17. About TV Viewing 44
18. Helpful Study Tips 46

19. Failure Redefined 49

20. Exam Anxiety 52

21. A Rational Approach to Challenging Negative Thoughts 58

22. Time Management 60

23. Case Study 62

24. Get Organized 64

25. Tips for Parents to Help Children Handle Exam Stress 67

26. SQ3RT – The Essence of Study Techniques 70

27. Value Yourself 72

28. About Anger 73

29. Parents' Guide to Encouraging a Child 77

Points to Ponder 81

PREFACE

Working with children has given me a completely new outlook towards several aspects of life, *schooling* being one of them. I have learnt a lot from them. I have come to understand our education system, children's views about this system, and of course about the "trauma" they experience regarding "studies". My interaction with students have been specially at a deep level. They share their innermost feelings, nightmares, fears and frustrations with me. I have accompanied children in their struggle during the exam time. Particularly as they reach higher classes like tenth standard or II P.U., they are simply distressed because of the pressure they go through. They are bombarded with instructions like *you must study well this year*, *I know you are intelligent, but it is just that you do not put in enough hard work* from all possible sources. While I understand the parents' anxiety, still I feel concerned for the children because they too are depressed, worried and nervous. I think the problem is that everyone wants them to study hard, but there is not enough guidance on how to study. As the saying goes, "It is not *how much* you study but *how* you study that counts." This book is an earnest effort to introduce some practical study skills.

Meera Ravi

A Special Word for Children

Dear Students

I understand that our education system is not the best one. Several children have told me that they find it extremely boring and tedious to sit through the monotonous classes. Some find the subjects very meaningless and the education system purposeless. I acknowledge your feelings of boredom and frustration, yet let me ask you, "Do we have a choice?" Can you say, "I don't want to be educated because I don't like the education system"? There is no alternative. It is this education which would get you a job in future and help you achieve your goal of becoming successful and earning money. Your dislike towards the education system or studies may be a truth, but the other truth remains that whether you like it or not, hating the system or cursing the studies is not going to get you anywhere. If you can accept this hard truth, it would become much easier for you. My only suggestion is to talk about your feelings with someone so you don't get overwhelmed.

I do not want to burden you with another book to '*study*', so I have tried my best to keep it simple and short. I have given some exercises which may help you understand yourself and build up your confidence. They are thought provoking, nevertheless simple. I am sure as you start doing them you would find them interesting. Once having done that, discuss it with someone trustworthy, either a close adult or a counsellor for a better understanding of yourself.

I forgot to make a backup copy of my brain, so everything I learned last week was lost.

1

KNOWING YOURSELF

Before we get down to talking about difficulties of study, let us first analyse what *your* specific difficulties are. Complete the following sentences with what you feel about the pressures from study, exams, school and parents. Talk about it with someone to overcome that difficulty.

- I am most comfortable when I am …
- I wish I had …
- I am most nervous when I …
- When I am tensed up, I tend to …
- I wish I did not have to …
- I know I am capable of …
- I dislike it when …
- My aim in life …
- I can concentrate much better if …
- I hate it when ...
- I get irritated when ...

2

Attitude

"The longer I live, the more I realize the impact of attitude on life.
Attitude to me is more important than facts.
It is more important than the past, than education, than money, than circumstance, than failure, than success, than what other people think or say or do.
It is more important than appearance, giftedness or skill.
It will make or break a company, a person, a home.
The remarkable thing is every day we have a choice regarding the attitude we will embrace for that day.
We cannot change our past. We cannot change the fact that people will act in a certain way.
We cannot change the inevitable.
The only thing we can do is play on the one string we do have, and that is our attitude ...
I am convinced that life is 10% what happens to me and 90% how I react to it.
And so is it with us. We are in charge of our attitudes."

Source: *Internet*

A study attributed to Harvard University found that when someone gets a job, 85% of the time it is on account of his attitude, and only 15% of the time because of how smart he is and how many facts and figures he knows.

We are either the masters or the victims of our attitudes. It is a matter of personal choice. Developing a **positive attitude** needs practice. Then it becomes a habit, and then part of one's character.

Once you develop a HABIT, it is very difficult to come out of it. When you put in some efforts to change the ~~H~~ABIT, A BIT of the habit remains. You put in some more effort, ~~A~~ BIT, BIT still remains. You try still harder ~~B~~IT, IT still remains. The habit still remains.

> *Do not develop bad habits. You get addicted to them and find it very difficult to give up the habits later.*

Positive attitude

Developing a positive attitude will lead you to happiness and success:

- Look at the bright side of life.
- Choose to be and stay optimistic.
- Focus on your good qualities and give yourself a pat on the back.
- Have faith in yourself.
- See problems as challenges and opportunities.
- Say "I can" more often than "I can't"
- Choose positive-thinking friends.
- Read inspiring stories/quotes.
- Repeat affirmations that inspire and motivate you.
- Learn to master your thoughts.

Our attitude toward life determines life's attitude toward us.

— John C. Maxwell

Attitude application challenge: For one week treat every person you meet, without a single exception, as the most important person on earth. You will find that they will begin treating you the same way!

Believe in yourself! Our **attitude** is the primary force that will determine whether we succeed or fail. The pessimist sees difficulty in every opportunity; the optimist finds an opportunity in every difficulty.

What does a **positive attitude** look like?

- You choose to look for the GOOD in people, situations, and yourself.
- You choose to be a GOOD SPORT.
- You choose to be PATIENTLY PERSISTENT. Do not give up easily!
- You choose to be GRATEFUL.

Positive mental attitude means having positive thoughts about people or situations.

"Miss, will you not provide a calculator to solve this?"

3

Having Positive Attitude When Things Go Wrong

It is no secret that life can be full of difficulties. Sometimes when things go wrong, it can seem almost impossible to maintain a positive attitude. If you are going through a difficult time and are starting to feel there is no way you can handle life's difficulties and maintain a positive attitude, then here are some easy ways to maintain a positive attitude.

Think of similar difficulties that resulted in a positive outcome

Think of other times when you have experienced a similar difficulty that resulted in a positive outcome. Ask yourself what you did then that made that difficult situation turn out OK for you. What specific things did you say or do to successfully overcome the same obstacle that you are facing again today? Remember your previous solutions.

Brainstorm

There is always a way out of a difficult situation, and you always have options, even if you do not know what they are when things suddenly go wrong. Take some time to sit down, relax, and brainstorm for some possible solutions. This will help you to feel less trapped, stuck, or overwhelmed; these are what most of us feel when we start to believe that we do not have options to remedy our problems in life. Reducing these common emotional responses will help you to think more clearly and choose a solution.

Choose a solution

After you have brainstormed for exploring various remedies for your problem, choose one solution. Choose the solution that sounds the most effective to you (select only one). Keep in mind that you are one step closer to resolving your difficult situation.

Take action

Take action. Be proactive and actualize your solution. By actually doing something about your problem instead of staying stuck in the disappointment, fear, or overwhelming mindset of your problem, you will begin to feel more hopeful and optimistic about your solution.

Focus on the solution instead of the problem

Stay focused on your solution and avoid dwelling on your problem. Your solution would most likely create joy, and your problem would most likely create unpleasant emotions that will be counterproductive to maintaining a positive attitude or resolving your problem. Stay focused, and do not lose hope.

Avoid telling yourself negative things

Avoid telling yourself negative things like "This is useless", "There is no hope", or "I'll never get through this". When you tell yourself negative things, it creates negative thinking – and negative thinking creates a negative attitude. Instead, tell yourself positive things like "I'm going to get through this" or "There is no problem that I cannot handle".

Maintaining a positive attitude all the time can be a difficult task. If you sense that your attitude could use a little adjusting, follow the tips given in the previous chapter.

> *There is very little difference between people, but that very little difference makes a big difference. The little difference is in attitude. The big difference is whether it is positive or negative.*

Are you a positive-thinking person?

Three things are needed to achieve success. Attitude, Skill and Knowledge (ASK). Very rightly, attitude is placed at the apex of the triangle because attitude is more important than knowledge and skill.

ATTITUDE
(Desire to perform)

KNOWLEDGE
(Can be acquired from books, authorities, education, observation)

SKILLS
(Can be developed by practice, experience)

IT IS NOT YOUR APTITUDE BUT YOUR ATTITUDE WHICH DECIDES YOUR ALTITUDE.

4

Why Study?

The most common question that students ask is "how to study?" Some also gather the courage to ask "why study?" If you have a *why*, the *hows* will come by.

The most important question that so many of us fail to ask is why we should study. Right from our childhood we are told to study. But we are rarely told the reason why we must study. And that is why so often most of us fail to achieve our academic goals.

A very dangerous idea is to study for scoring high marks. This will put you in the purely competitive lane, and you will judge your progress solely by your marks. Remember not to hype up your marks – they just will tell you how you are doing. People fail to realize this simple fact that marks are nothing more than your performance index. To improve your marks you need to improve your performance.

One of the most important objectives of study is a career. A degree ensures that you get a job when your grow up or you will have a sufficient knowledge to operate your own business. **In fact the best of the degrees ensure a smooth life.** That is one of the reasons why you must study. Remember even if you do not study, you will be able to earn, but you will be dependent and will have to work harder. There can be many other reasons, but in my opinion education must be pursued for knowledge – for the pure worship of knowledge. Education builds up your character and refines your soul.

To know the true value of education, ask someone who is illiterate and you will realize the immense value of something you have been taking for granted.

> *Make a list of at least five strong reasons why you have to study. Paste them somewhere you can see, and read them frequently.*

5

Introduction to Study Techniques

Before we get to these tips, however, there are two very important points to consider. The first is that there is no right or wrong way to study. Each of us is an individual and each of us will find something a little different that works. Your study plan may differ from that of your best friend or from that of your own brother. The trick is to figure out what works best for you and then stick to it.

Secondly, you as the student are the person most responsible for doing your work. You must decide to study for yourself, not for someone else's sake. No amount of tips would help if you were not motivated to study.

Learning would be great fun if we didn't have to study so much.

6

Case Study

Kalpana was coming to the end of her first year of B.Com. Throughout the year she had been depressed and anxious every time she was required to take an exam. Though she scored very well and was a topper, she did not think that was good enough. Kalpana had very few friends and did not have any hobby. She had studied and studied to prove that she was worthy of her parents' sacrifices in encouraging her. She realized that as the year went on, her concentration seemed poorer when she was revising. She was becoming increasingly nervous during exams. For instance, at the beginning of an exam, her hand shook so much that she had to struggle to hold her pen. In addition, her mouth went dry, her stomach felt knotted, her mind felt empty and she was afraid of fainting.

A certain amount of anxiety is common during exams. Anxiety tones up and facilitates performance. However, in Kalpana's case too much of anxiety had become debilitating in terms of both discomfort and poor performance.

Here are some tips for Kalpana to work on her exam-anxiety problems. She must ask herself

Am I in touch with my primary feelings?

She does not realize she is out of touch with her own valuing process. She does not recognize her basic needs of recreation and social companionships. It might help if Kalpana does deeper introspection and identifies what her actual feelings are. For you to know what is happening inside you, I would like you to fill up the following as accurately as you can.

Take a sheet of paper and do this exercise on that.

- I feel anxious because
- I feel afraid
- I feel frustrated
- I feel irritated
- I feel confused
- I feel happy
- I feel tensed up
- I feel angry when

Once you have done this, go to the next step and write down what specifically about them makes you feel so. This is another very important aspect of self-awareness. Unless you know what you are feeling, you wouldn't know what to do about it.

Who set the rules for me and are they helping me?

Kalpana is making impractical demands on herself. She has oppressing personal rules "I must do extremely well every time I take an exam", "I must always obtain my parents' approval". She engages in unnecessary self-rating: "If I do not do well, then I am a worthless person." She feels, "If I do not do well, this is an awful disaster I will not be able to handle." It is possible that adults around her tuned her to have these rules for her. It might help if she reconsiders the rules.

Are my perceptions accurate regarding others and myself?

Kalpana needs to explore her academic abilities realistically. She may be a brilliant student, but extreme anxiety has become a hindrance to her achievement. On the top of it she has unrealistic expectations from herself. Rational analysis of available facts regarding her academic strengths and weaknesses will help her perceive herself more accurately. She needs to test her own perception of her parents.

Are my explanations accurate?

Kalpana is overworking because she makes inaccurate conclusions about why she is not doing well. She regards any "failure" on her part as due to lack of effort. She needs to review whether there are "better fit" explanations for her not performing as well as she would like in some exams. Explanations could include **insufficient ability, lack of interest in the subject, poor teaching, emotional disturbance, poor revision skills, high anxiety.**

Evaluate yourself on each and every question that is described in the case of Kalpana.

7

ANXIETY QUIZ

- Do you usually feel jittery or tense?
- Do you worry a great deal?
- Do you have unrealistic fears?
- Are you unable to relax?
- Are your hands cold and sweaty?
- Do you have difficulty concentrating?
- Are you often irritable and restless?
- Do you have palpitations at the thought of exams?
- Do you sometimes have tingling in your hands and feet?
- Are you often impatient?

If you have answered yes to some of these questions, you may be overtly anxious, and if it persists, it is advisable to talk to someone.

8

General Tips

Two biggest enemies of a student who wants to score well are:

- Bad handwriting
- Poor spelling

It is never too late to begin anything. If you feel your handwriting is not good enough, spend fifteen minutes a day to develop speed in writing that is also neat and legible. Try improving the spelling too, identifying what are the kinds of spellings you find difficult. It is worth putting in extra effort, as it will bring returns in the long run. In your spare time read as much as possible, be it newspaper, magazines or story books. This would also help you in improving your vocabulary. Try to learn five new words and their meanings every week.

Wrong study habits

- Reading without understanding
- No review/recall exercises
- Last-hour preparation
- Severe performance anxiety
- Poor time management
- Poor self-confidence
- Emotional distress

My friends crack jokes and make me laugh in the class. I get easily distracted.

You cannot change others or stop them from cracking jokes, but you can surely control your behaviour. Use your willpower and make up your mind not to get diverted. Remember if you choose to get distracted, you will get punishment, you will lose concentration, and finally you will be a loser. Try this method sincerely. Out of every five times the jokes are cracked, even if once you are able to ignore them, be proud of the achievement. That will motivate you to be strong-willed in future.

9

CONCENTRATION

Concentration has been defined as "the ability to direct one's thinking in whatever direction one would intend".

We all have the ability to concentrate for some time. But at other times our thoughts are scattered, and our minds race from one thing to another. To deal with such times, you need to learn and practise concentration skills and strategies. To concentrate, you have to learn a skill, and as with any skill this means practising it repeatedly day after day until you achieve enough improvement to feel that you can concentrate when you need to.

Look at the following familiar scene

You need to study something for your forthcoming exam. You sit comfortably on the sofa with the book in your hands and start reading. After a while you feel hungry and go to the kitchen to eat something.

You return to read, and then you hear people talking outside. You listen to them for several moments and then bring your attention back to the book.

After a while you feel restless and switch on the radio to listen to some music. You continue to read for a little while, and then remember something that happened yesterday in the class, and you start thinking about it.

When you look at your watch, you are amazed to find out that one complete hour has passed and you have hardly read anything.

This is what happens when concentration is not strong enough to ward off all disturbances. There are many situations in life where a little concentration can make a great difference. Think, and you will find out many such situations. Imagine what you could have accomplished, if you possessed even just a little of this ability!

Work that requires physical strength, such as carrying heavy loads for example, develops physical strength. Yet, it is not like exercising daily in the gym in a systematic manner. The same applies to concentration. Reading, studying and trying to pay attention to what we do develop some of this ability, but practising exercises diligently each day is something else, it is like training in a gym.

The main barriers to concentrating are boredom, anxiety and day-dreaming. Thus in improving your concentration skills you need to counteract these barriers. The following three skills are basic to concentration: if you want to improve your concentration, start by practising them. They will be followed by further strategies which will allow you to build onto the basic skills.

1. Stop!

This sounds very simple, but it works. When you notice your thoughts wandering, say to yourself STOP and then gently bring your attention back to where you want it to be. An alternative method is visualizing the traffic signal 'STOP' every time you want to stop your thoughts from wandering.

Each time it wanders bring it back. To begin with, this could be several times a minute. But each time, say STOP and then re-focus. Don't waste energy trying to keep thoughts out of your mind (forbidden thoughts attract like a magnet!), just put the effort into STOP and re-focus.

To begin with, you will do this hundreds of times a week. And you will find that the period of time between your straying thoughts gets a little longer each day, so be patient and keep at it.

2. Attending

This is about maintaining concentration and not giving in to distractions. It could be described as a sort of tunnel-vision, or as being focused: you keep your concentration on what is in front of you. If you are distracted, use the STOP technique to regain concentration. You can practise attending in many situations:

- In a class, if other students move or laugh, ignore them, don't look at them, actively exclude them from the link or tunnel formed between you and the teacher.
- In a social situation, keep your attention solely on one person – what he says, how he looks, etc. – and ignore what is going on around you.

3. Worry time

Set aside one or more specific periods in the day when you are allowed to worry. It can help to set them just before something that you know you will do, to ensure that you stop worrying on time – e.g. before a favourite TV programme, or a meal-time. Whenever an anxiety or distracting thought enters your mind during the day, banish it until your next worry time, and re-focus on what you are supposed to be doing. Some students find it helpful to write down the banished thought: it is easier to send away a thought if you are sure you won't have forgotten it when you get to your worry time. It is important that you keep your worry time(s), and make yourself worry for the full time. If you find that you can't fill the time available, then make a conscious decision to reduce it.

You may notice, particularly if you keep a list, that certain things keep reappearing: this is a fairly clear indication that you need to do something about them! May be talk to a counsellor about them and get it out of your mind.

A number of students have tried the above technique and they have told me it has worked very well for them. Do give it a try sincerely.

Other things that can help:

- Once you know what your concentration span is for a specific activity, decide whether it is acceptable or whether you need to train yourself to expand it.
- In between periods of concentration, do things to change your physical and mental activity – e.g. move around to boost your circulation if you have been sitting, give your brain a new focus.
- Give yourself incentives and rewards appropriate to the level of concentration you have had to maintain.
- Ensure that your environment aids concentration – reduce distractions and don't be so comfortable that you nod off.
- Do tasks that need most concentration at times when you are mentally and physically fresh: concentration is harder to maintain when you are tired. This means you need to know the times of the day when you work best. This time differs from person to person.
- Experiment and see whether working with another person helps you keep focused on the task.
- If you feel stuck check if the problem is one of poor concentration rather than lack of necessary knowledge or understanding.

The power of concentration

I am now going to give you some simple exercises to perform. Start with five minutes each day, and in time you may lengthen the time to fifteen minutes. Do you know that the mind does not like any discipline? It loves its freedom more than anything else, and will try to stand in your way, whenever and however it can. It will cause you to forget to do the exercises, make you feel lazy, and tempt you to postpone the exercises. It will find many tricks to stop and disturb you, but you can and must be stronger.

Before the concentration exercises

When starting to learn to concentrate you have to find a place where you can be alone and undisturbed. You can sit cross-legged on the floor if you can, or on a chair. Sit with spine erect. Take a few calm deep breaths and then relax your body. In your mind go through each muscle and part of the body and relax it.

I will now give you some exercises to practise. Start with the first exercise, and practise it daily, until you are able to do it easily and without thinking about anything else for at least five minutes. You have to be honest with yourself, and proceed to the next one only after you are convinced that the exercise is practised with full concentration.

No timetable can be given, as this may be frustrating. If for example I tell you that an exercise has to be completed in a week, two things may happen. You may get disappointed if you cannot get the desired concentration within a week, or you may move on without practising the exercise correctly. Practising an exercise successfully is an individual matter. It may take days, weeks and sometimes even months.

Put your whole attention into the exercises. Do not think about anything else. Be careful not to fall asleep, daydream or think about other matters. The moment you find yourself thinking about something else, stop the exercise and start again. You may think the exercises are too simple and easy and try to perform them all at once. Go slowly, do not overdo or tense you brain. Remember that everyone encounters difficulties along the way. The successful ones are those who go on and never give up.

It does not matter if your concentration is weak, it can be strengthened. You need not be some special person to be able to do that. But each will reach a different level of concentration. Some will have a stronger power, others not so strong. It all depends on how much time, energy and earnestness you put into the project. I repeat what I wrote earlier, even five minutes a day will add to your power.

In time you will find out that you can concentrate anywhere, anytime, no matter what your circumstances are.

Now to the exercises. Some of them may be familiar to you. Some may seem too easy to perform. Some were taken from various sources and some created by me. When your concentration and knowledge about concentration increases you will be able to create new exercises by yourself.

Concentration exercises

Exercise 1

Take a book and count the words in any one paragraph. Count them again to be sure that you have counted them correctly. Start with one paragraph and when it becomes easier, count the words in a whole page. Perform the counting mentally and only with your eyes, without pointing your finger at each word.

Exercise 2

Count backwards in your mind, from one hundred to one.

Exercise 3

Count in your mind from one hundred to one, skipping each three numbers, that is 100, 97, 94, etc.

Exercise 4

Choose an inspiring word, or just a simple sound, and repeat it silently in your mind for five minutes. When your mind can concentrate more easily, try to reach ten minutes of uninterrupted concentration.

Exercise 5

Take a fruit, an apple for example, and look at it from all sides. Concentrate your attention on it and examine it from all sides. Devote the whole session to concentrating on it. Do not be carried away by irrelevant thoughts that arise. Stay with the apple. It could be any other fruit. Look at it and do not think about the shop where you bought it, about the way it is grown, its nutritive value, etc., only about the object in front of you. Just look at it, see it, smell it and touch it. Difficult? Doesn't matter. Don't give up. Practise it.

Exercise 6

This is the same as exercise number 5, only that this time you visualize the fruit with your eyes closed. Start by performing again exercise number 5 for five minutes, and then do this one. Try to see, feel, taste, smell the fruit in you imagination. Try to see a clear and well-defined image. If difficulties arise open your eyes, look at the fruit, close them again and continue the exercise.

The secret of success is constant practice. The more time you devote to the exercises the faster your success arrives. Go on gradually; ten minutes at the start and in time as you gain the ability to concentrate, give it more time. When you see that you are successful, you will begin to love the exercises, and in time they will become a habit. You will be able to concentrate your attention easily and effortlessly upon anything you want to concentrate on.

Additional tips

- Set aside a place where you will study that has minimum distraction. Eliminate any distractions that you can, and make the environment comfortable.
- Ensure that your study area has the following
  - Good lighting
  - Ventilation
  - A comfortable chair, but not comfortable enough to doze off.
  - A desk large enough to spread out your materials.
- Ensure that your study area does not have the following
  - A distracting view of the other activities that you want to be involved in
  - A telephone
  - A stereo
  - TV
  - A roommate or friend who talks a lot

- Make sure you have all your material when you sit down to study. This may include pencils, pens, calculator, textbooks, paper, etc.
- "Pencil Technique": always study with a pencil in your hand. Rewrite what you have read, your notes, key points and questions.
- Set time limit and stop studying before you are too tired to achieve the best concentration and retention.
- Vary the activity–read for a while, then take some notes or change subject of study.
- Take a break.

Try to reduce any tension you may be having. If something is worrying you, first sort it out. ***Mental disturbance*** *is one of the* ***biggest hindrances*** *to* ***concentration****.*

10

EMOTIONAL DISTURBANCE

The most important way of dealing with emotional disturbance is to identify the feeling. Whenever you feel disturbed about something, try to identify what that feeling is. This chart would help you in identifying the feeling. Once you have identified the feeling, ask yourself the following questions.

- Who is responsible for this feeling?
- Have I felt like this before? If yes, when?
- What are the events that triggered off this feeling?
- To whom can I talk about it?
- Have there been similar events when others made me feel like this?
- How did I overcome that?

Sometimes children come to me and ask for 'concentration tips', I help them out with that. After a few days they come back and say, "Ma'am I used those tips; it worked for 3–4 days but now again I am not able to concentrate." The reason is usually they are disturbed about certain things and despite best efforts they are not able to concentrate well. Then I encourage them to talk about their feelings.

So in this regard I would like to suggest that you talk about it. Believe me, this is one of the major barriers in having good concentration. If your mind is upset or you are disturbed about something, it is likely that it would keep bothering you until you share it with someone. Many children share with me that when they have a fight with a sibling or a friend or when they have got some kind of punishment or had a bad experience, the thoughts of these keep disturbing them while they try to study. I encourage them to talk about their experience and I address their negative feelings. If you have too many negative feelings it becomes difficult to have a calm mind. You may read books and get study skills but if your mind itself is disturbed, you may not be able to apply the skills.

Think for example if you are being teased with a girl or a boy, how would you feel? You may feel embarrassed, angry, helpless and/or lonely. If you keep all these feelings within you, it would keep distracting your mind and you cannot learn at a pace you would want to.

Let me explain much more simply. If you have a glass full of water, can you fill more water in it? If you want to fill more water, you have to pour some water out, empty the glass a little and then fill more water. It is the same with your mind. If your mind is full of negative thoughts, new learning cannot find place, you have to pour out the negativity to make place for learning.

So for the process of learning to take place smoothly, I suggest, don't bottle up feelings. Share them with someone, unburden yourself and experience the calmness.

No one understands me.

They say I am stupid.

I think nobody loves me.

Dignity/ Respect/ Self-Worth	***Freedom/ Control***	***Love/Connection/ Importance***	***Justice/Truth***	***Safety***	***Trust***
Ashamed	Bossed around	Abandoned	Accused	Abused	Cynical
Beaten down	Controlled	Alone	Cheated	Afraid	Guarded
Cut down	Imprisoned	Brushed off	Falsely accused	Attacked	Skeptical
Criticized	Inhibited	Confused	Guilt-tripped	Frightened	Suspicious
Dehumanized	Forced	Disapproved of	Interrogated	Intimidated	Untrusting
Disrespected	Manipulated	Discouraged	Judged	Over-protected	
Embarrassed	Obligated	Ignored	Lied about	Scared	
Humiliated	Over-controlled	Insignificant		Terrified	
Insulted	Over-ruled	Invisible			
Inferior	Powerless	Left out			
Invalidated	Pressured	Lonely			
Labelled		Misunderstood			
Lectured to		Neglected			
Mocked		Rejected			
Offended		Uncared for			
Put down		Unheard			
Resentful		Unknown			
Ridiculed		Unloved			

Please do not ignore or negate any feeling. Try and identify the feeling, and if it is overwhelming, talk to someone about it. Bottled-up feelings would sabotage your learning.

11

Memory Tips

There is nothing such as a good memory or a bad memory. Biologically all of us have the same brains – and even then when you see the marks people get in an exam, no two people get exactly identical marks. The difference is due to a trained and an untrained memory.

Understand the subject matter: Unless you understand the matter, you cannot remember it.

Repetition: Repeat the whole, often using the "eye-gate" by looking at it attentively, and "ear-gate" by repeating it aloud. Spread out the repetition over a number of days. Repeating after some hours and days makes it sink deeper into your memory.

Frequent review: Studying new information on the same day you heard or read it helps. It is likely to improve memory significantly. A small review each day is essential if you have memory problems.

Colour code: By using colouring pens, highlighters, post-it notes and flags, you can make an impression on your memory. This is a way of sorting information for storage as you assign colours.

Rehearse aloud: Verbal rehearsal is an effective memory tool.

Get enough sleep: Lack of sleep has negative effects on your ability to remember.

Take breaks while studying: You will not be so tired, and you can focus better.

The basic requirement is interest. Pick up a subject of your interest and see how much you remember. For example, if it is cricket, see how many cricketers' names you can list. You will be amazed at the result, especially for sports, movies and other interesting fields.

Please note:

- There are no medicines, tonics, health drinks to improve learning memory or performance in the examination.
- Good physical and mental health, good motivation and study habits, high self-esteem and confidence help to improve learning memory.
- A stress-free mind is where learning takes place.

Reasons why breaks make students work better

1. Breaks make learning pleasant. It is relatively easy to sit down to study when you know it is for a limited period of time.
2. Breaks refresh your mind and help you concentrate better, and when you take a break even when you are not tired, you are actually taking preventive action.
3. Breaks set a goal indirectly. You will be forced to finish a portion before the deadline.
4. Research shows that students concentrate best at the beginning and at the end of the study session. Breaks create more beginnings and ends.
5. Breaks teach discipline and self-control.
6. Breaks create an opportunity to revise. After your break, it is useful to run through earlier material.

Are you sure there is no 'serious' talking after this treat?

12

THE POWER OF *'ATTENTION'*

We all know that attention is a very desirable skill, but how many possess it? I don't need to tell you why it is important, and what are its uses and benefits. You must have heard it many a time, "So and so is very intelligent but he does not pay attention. . . " Or "If only you paid more attention in the class. . ." such comments are very common to hear. Good attention is a must for every person who desires to succeed, whether on a minor or a major scale. In order to gain success you need to be able to focus your mind, and to calm down its restlessness and tendency to constantly shift from one subject to another.

Every act needs attention for its successful performance. Working, talking, conversing, studying and playing require attention. In fact I feel that even basic chores like washing, cleaning the house or cooking require it, in order to be handled efficiently.

People are born with certain power of attention which has to be developed over years. There are times when the attention becomes very strong, though involuntarily, and without exercising real control over it. Think of the times when you watch a thriller movie or when you are reading a captivating book. What happens? You are so absorbed that you are disconnected from the outside world. This usually happens when we engage in activities that we enjoy and love.

Developing the power of attention

For this ability to be useful, it should be under the control of your will. You have to be able to decide where and when to focus your mind. Every day you are presented with plenty of opportunities to strengthen the power of your attention. Actually, every action can be turned into an exercise. Hold your mind on whatever you do, and try to concentrate without deviating to something else. It is true that special concentration exercises are necessary, but if you cannot find the time and place to perform them, you can turn the whole day into an enjoyable exercise. Focus on whatever you do, and in time your ability would increase.

In this way you will not only strengthen your attention and concentration, but everything you do will be done better, more efficiently, and even faster. In time, as your attention gets stronger, thoughts will lose their power to distract you, and you will find that you can absorb yourself in whatever you do. This will increase your efficiency, and make you enjoy whatever you do.

Here are a few suggestions for developing and strengthening the power of attention:

- When reading a book, focus your eyes and mind on the words, and do not to think of anything not connected with what you are reading. Ignore outside noises and any irrelevant thoughts.
- Whatever you are doing, reading newspaper, dressing up, playing, or watching TV, put your whole attention on your movements.
- When you are doing a particular job, say setting the table for dinner, clearing the table, cleaning your room, concentrate on each act and movement, without daydreaming or thinking about something else.

- While walking or engaging in any kind of physical activity, don't daydream or think on whatever enters your mind. Instead, focus your attention on what you are doing.
- While conversing, listen attentively to what people are saying.
- While eating, focus your mind on your food and on enjoying it.
- Always do one thing at a time.

The gist of the whole thing is BE AWARE of yourself and your movements.

You don't have to do all the above, all the time. Even a few minutes now and then will do wonders for you, and develop your power of attention. Persevere, and you will gain a very useful ability, which will help you on many occasions in your life.

13

Some Introspection

One of the most common statements I hear from many children is, "I had studied so well Ma'am, but despite that I got very less marks in the last test."

First of all I would like to say that 'less' is a relative term. Let me ask you a few questions:

Is it less than what *you* expected or less than what *someone else* expected?

Whoever it is, on what basis were the expectations set?

Was it a realistic expectation?

Secondly I would like to ask you to do a post-mortem analysis, when you say, "I had studied so well. . ." Think about it, what happened, why you got *'less'* marks. According to you what was the reason?

- Did you find the question paper too lengthy and you couldn't complete answering it? *If 'yes' then for the next time you can solve more past exam papers and practise answering questions within the allotted time.*
- Did you have to leave out some questions without attempting to answer because you did not know the answers? *In that case, you will have to re-evaluate your preparation.*
- Do you think the question paper was out of portion? *Though I think this would be a rare possibility, still if you think this was the reason, then from next time you can make sure about the portions to study. (In any case if this is true then everyone would get affected.)*

- Did you become nervous while taking the exam? *Then think about it, what specifically was the nervousness about? Was it that you would not be able to score as much as your parents expect or was it that you would not get the expected rank or was it that you would fail? The next step is to think if your expectation is realistic.*
- Do you think your answers were not complete or enough to score well? *Does it reflect on your preparation? Next time make sure you prepare well where you are lacking this time.*

This kind of post-mortem analysis will help you identify where things went wrong this time so that you can correct it for the next time. If you are not aware of it, then there is a possibility that you may keep doing the same mistake again. It is very important to know where you need to bring in changes in your study methods or your expectation.

A word of caution: Don't be hasty in finding a reason. If you are not comfortable, you don't have to share the above exercise with anyone, just be honest with yourself. At the end of this exercise if you realize that you were partially responsible for it or it was your miscalculation, don't brood over it. Mistakes happen. It is okay to make mistakes; the wisdom is in correcting the mistake next time.

14

Why Procrastinate?

Procrastination is the habit of putting tasks off to the last possible minute. It can be a major problem in both your academics and your personal life. Let's explore the root causes of procrastination and give you several practical tools to overcome it.

I am sure despite best intentions, you get tempted to delay sitting for studies. You must be going through that phase when you do not want to make the effort to start because you feel tired, lazy or just bored. I have met countless children who criticize themselves for putting off their work. And they have given me different reasons why they do so. I would like to share some of their reasons:

- It gives me satisfaction to go against the system.
- I study better under pressure.
- With last hour preparation, I can retain better.
- It saves me from revision.
- Studying is so unpleasant; I want to do least.
- Anyway it is not going to make a difference in my marks, so why study more?

You may even have thought up more excuses. Whatever these are, they are safer out in the open than keeping them in your mind. Once you understand why you resist studying, you can criticize yourself less for it. Also having these reasons out in the open gives you a chance to challenge them.

The reasons why I procrastinate. . .

1.

2.

3.

You may even think that it is boring/difficult to study. What will happen ultimately if you continue procrastinating? Give it a thought.

The simple cure? Do everything opposite. Tell yourself: 'this isn't so hard', 'it is not as boring as I thought it would be'. 'I am sure that I know how to do it, or 'I am sure that I can learn while I'm doing it'. This kind of talking to yourself would help.

1. Try self-reassurance that this effort will be good enough,
2. Make an effort to appreciate what you have done.

There is another important cause of lack of motivation. If you are angry, frustrated or upset about anything, it would affect your motivation level. That is why also earlier in the book I have talked about 'emotional disturbance' (chapter 10) and have given a list of feelings. It is extremely important to be in touch with your feelings and talk about them to someone.

15

Willpower

Willpower is the ability to control unnecessary and harmful impulses. It is the ability to overcome laziness and procrastination. It is the ability to arrive at a decision and follow it with perseverance until its successful accomplishment. It is the inner power that overcomes the desire to indulge in unnecessary and useless habits.

Willpower helps us to choose our behaviour and reactions instead of being their slaves. How many times have you felt too weak, lazy or shy to do something you wanted to do? You can gain inner strength, initiative and the ability to make decisions and follow them. Believe me, it is not difficult to develop this power. If you are earnest and are willing to become stronger, you will certainly succeed.

I will give you some exercises and techniques for developing these abilities. These simple, but effective exercises can be performed everywhere, and at any time. Go slowly and gradually, and you will see how you get stronger and your life improves. By practising appropriate exercises, you develop your powers the same way as a person who trains the muscles in order to strengthen them.

Developing willpower

One way to develop and improve these abilities is to practise doing some disagreeable things in your daily life. Your mind and feelings will probably oppose doing them, nevertheless, do them. Let me explain. By doing something you do not like or are too lazy to do, you overcome your subconscious resistances, train your inner powers and gain inner strength. Muscles get stronger by resisting the power of the barbells. Inner strength is attained by overcoming inner resistance.

Remember, strengthening one of these abilities automatically strengthens the other ones.

Here are a few exercises:

1. You are sitting in a bus or train and an old man or woman, or a woman with an infant walks in. Stand up and give up your seat even if you prefer to stay seated. Do this not just because it is polite, but because you are doing something that you are reluctant to do. In this way you are overcoming the resistance of your body, mind and feelings.
2. There are lots of clothes to iron, and you postpone ironing them for later. Get up and iron them now. Do not let your laziness overcome you. When you know that in this way you are developing your willpower, and if you are convinced of the importance of willpower in your life, it will be easier for you to do whatever you have to do.
3. You come home tired from tuition and sit in front of the T.V. because you feel too lazy and tired to go and have a wash. Do not obey the desire to just sit, but go and have a shower.
4. You may know your body needs some physical exercise, but instead you keep on sitting doing nothing or watching a movie. Get up and go for a walk, run or do some other physical exercise.
5. Do you like your coke a lot and drink five–six glasses a day? Then for a whole week decide to drink only one glass a day.
6. Overcome your laziness and your habits. Convince yourself of the importance of what is to be done. Convince

your mind that you become stronger when you do things even when you are reluctant, too lazy or believe you are too tired to do.

7. Sometimes, when you want to say something that is not important, decide not to say it.
8. You love to read the gossip about the film stars in the newspaper. For ten days, don't read it.
9. You have a desire to eat something not too healthy like chaat or pani puri. Refuse the desire.
10. If you find yourself thinking unimportant, unnecessary, negative thoughts, try to develop lack of interest in them, by thinking about their futility.

Never say that you cannot follow the above exercises, because you certainly can. Be persistent no matter what. Motivate yourself by thinking about the importance of performing the exercises, and the inner power and strength you will gain.

Trying to attempt too many exercises when you are still a beginner might end in disappointment. It is better to start training yourself through easier exercises at first, and gradually increase the number and difficulty of the exercises. Practice will improve and increase your power, giving you a lot of satisfaction.

Most of these exercises can be practised anywhere, anytime. You do not have to devote special time for them. Believe me, they are very effective. Practising them enables you to be strong and exercise willpower and self-discipline in everything you do. This power becomes available whenever needed.

If you practise weightlifting, running or doing aerobics, you strengthen your body. When you need to move something heavy, you have the strength for it. The same thing happens with willpower and self-discipline. By strengthening them, they become available whenever they are needed.

It is important to remember not to choose exercises that might adversely affect your body or health. Deny and give up what is not necessary, futile or is harmful,

but not what is vital for your well being. Always use your reason and common sense, so that you do no damage to yourself.

If for the sake of an exercise you stop doing something that you usually do, and overcome the inner resistance concerning it, you may resume doing it, if it is not harmful. For example, if you love drinking orange juice, and for the sake of an exercise you switch to drinking apple juice, after doing so for some time and after it makes no great difference for you, you may go back to drinking orange juice, if you still like it. **The point here is to develop inner strength, not make life difficult for you and continue doing things you don't like to do.**

> *Important note: whenever you are successful in pushing yourself against a particular desire and feel that you used your willpower, give yourself a pat on the back.*

16

GROUP STUDY – SOME GUIDELINES

It is generally recognized that people can accomplish more by sharing their skills and resources than by working alone. We even have a saying, "Two heads are better than one" to demonstrate this phenomenon. Here are a few pointers for setting up a study group.

1. Select people who seem to share your desire to reach your academic goals.
2. Look for people who stay alert in the class, who take notes, ask questions, who respond to the teacher's questions. Even if they are not very close friends, it is OK. You may learn new thing and ways of study with new people.
3. Limit your group to four to six people, larger groups get cumbersome and small groups can too easily get off track.
4. Schedule a meeting to "test the waters" and see how you get along together. Once the group seems to be doing well, try to schedule regular meetings.
5. Take turns "teaching" each other the material. If you have to teach a concept, you really have to know that concept,

so you are not only helping others but also reinforcing your own knowledge.

6. Make sure someone takes the role of a session leader to keep the session productive.
7. Compare notes.
8. Take a few minutes at the end of the session to evaluate what you have done. Did everyone put in his or her full effort? Did we concentrate too much on one topic? How can we improve our efforts?
9. Plan the next meeting. Give the group assignments.

Once back home, introspect and analyse yourself. Am I comfortable in the group? Am I learning more in a group? Is it worth studying in a group? Will I be saving time if I did not have to go anywhere?

Studying together the wrong way

"Let's get together and study for that big maths exam next week," says your best friend Tara. A good idea! Maybe, maybe not. But if you follow the method as described below, then be sure that you will be **totally lost when you appear for your exam!**

- Tell her to come to your house **whenever she can**. Maybe you will be watching TV or reading a novel, but that would be OK.
- When she does come, start out by telling her you will get started in just a minute, but first you just have to tell her the rumour you heard about another common friend. Maybe she will have some rumours to share, too.
- Skip your last meal beforehand. That way you will be able to have a continuous snack attack during your study time.
- Turn on your favourite TV programme. You can still study while you watch the show, right?

- Ask your other friend to call you while Tara is there, so you can both talk to her. Ditto for Shilpa, Amala and whoever else you can think of.
- Forget to collect your Math class work from a classmate.

Think of five people who can be part of your study group. What are the topics that can be best studied as a group?

17

ABOUT TV VIEWING

I know I shouldn't be watching too much of TV, but I just can't get up and go.

Let me begin by saying you are not the only one who experiences this. I have heard countless children complaining about the TV addiction. Let's first admit that TV is indeed tempting. It is easier said than done to leave such interesting and entertaining stuff and sit for studies. Yet think about it. If you continue to watch TV, what would happen?

Use the extra sheets given at the end of the book and make two columns. On one side you write the advantages of watching TV, on the other side write the disadvantages.

Be honest while doing this exercise. You do not have to show it to anyone. Do it for yourself. Then decide what you want to do. **Remember that you are responsible for the choice you make.**

I lose track of the time when I am watching TV. Then I realize I have wasted a lot of time.

First make up your mind that you sincerely want to do something about it. Once you are determined, then try any of the following methods to fight the battle against the "devil".

- Set an alarm for the time when you want to switch off the TV.
- Ask someone to remind you to get up. It could be an adult or even a younger sibling or cousin.
- Invite three or four friends to join you to fight this battle with the "devil". Set a time limit for watching TV, and promise each other that you would watch only that much. Next day share your experience with each other.
- Fix up the time to watch TV for six days in a week. Pamper yourself with extra TV watching one day. But make sure you pamper yourself only if you have truthfully followed the six-days' timetable.

Take it as a challenge to find innovative ways of fighting your battle against TV. Most importantly, give yourself a pat every time you are able to win against your temptation.

Eventually it is your willpower that is going to liberate you from this monster. Some children tell me they do not have any willpower, and I disagree with them. All of us have the determination, but we use it selectively.

Think of the incidents in the past (whether concerning studies or not) when you used your willpower and won over a situation.

18

HELPFUL STUDY TIPS

There are as many different ways to study as there are people. The trick is to find the study tips that work best for you. The following is a list of tips that have worked best for the greatest number of people. Some of them may work for you, some of them may not, but try them all and work out your own study plan.

Study in the same place

Find a quiet place, away from distractions, with ample room to work. Once you have found it, study at the same place every time. Lying down on your bed or sprawled across the living room rug are generally not good postures for study.

Study at the same time

Figure out what time of the day you can concentrate best and what works into your schedule. Use that time every day to study. Try to make sure you do not deprive yourself of sleep.

Be organized

Keep all your books in one place. Keep them organized, and you will not need to waste your time searching for them.

Cut out all distractions

You need to be able to concentrate on your homework and nothing else. The TV should be off, other people's conversations should be in another room, music should be turned down, and phone calls should be taken after you have finished studying. Any other thoughts in your mind should also be set aside for a later time.

Do the tough subject first

If you are dreading a particular subject, or know it requires a lot of extra effort, study it first. Your brain will be fresh at the time of commencement. Besides, you will not have to dwell on it while you are working on some other homework.

Review regularly

A regular review of your notes should be a part of your study plan. This takes just a few minutes each day, but will pay off considerably when it comes to test time.

Write up a contract

Write up a contract at the beginning of each term with yourself. This sets out in writing what is your commitment towards your studies. You must keep up this commitment with yourself.

Schedule each study session

When you sit down to study, make up a quick schedule as to how you are going to use your time. Break it up into small blocks of time that you will spend on each task.

Avoid doing last minute preparation

If you have followed the previous tips, this last one should never happen. You need to know that marathon study sessions are the least productive way to study.

19

Failure Redefined

Here is a new perspective on failure you must internalize, and you will never have any failure in your life.

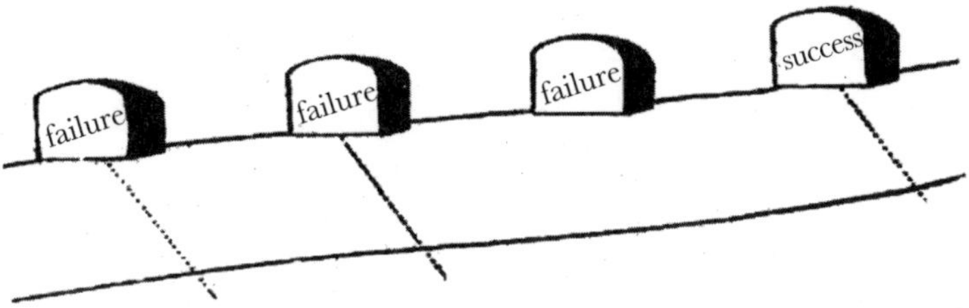

With every failure you are nearer to success.

Failure does not mean	**Failure means**
You are a failure.	You have not succeeded.
You have accomplished nothing.	You have learnt something.
You will never be able to do.	You have to do it in a different way.
You are inferior.	You are not perfect.
You have wasted your life.	You have to start afresh.
You should give up.	You should try harder.
You will never achieve.	You may take longer.

Do you call them failures?

- Thomas Edison was partially deaf, and he had only three months of formal schooling. His teacher said he was too stupid to learn anything.
- Isaac Newton did very poorly in school.
- Leo Tolstoy, author of *War and Peace*, flunked out of college; he was described as "both unable and unwilling to learn".
- A newspaper editor fired Walt Disney because he thought Walt Disney lacked ideas. He also went bankrupt several times before he built Disneyland.
- Henry Ford failed and went bankrupt five times before he finally succeeded. In the first car that he made, he forgot to install reverse gear.
- Winston Churchill failed in sixth grade.
- Beethoven handled the violin awkwardly and preferred playing his own compositions instead of improving his techniques. His teacher called him hopeless as a composer.
- Charles Darwin, father of the Theory of Evolution, gave up medical career. In his autobiography he says, "I was considered by all my masters and also by my father as a very ordinary boy, rather below the common standard in intellect."
- Alexander Graham Bell was desperately trying to invent a hearing aid for his partially deaf wife. He failed at that; however, he discovered the principle of telephone.
- Albert Einstein did not speak until he was four years old and did not read until he was seven. His teacher described him as "mentally slow, unsociable and adrift, and for ever in his foolish dreams." He was expelled and was refused admission to the Zurich Polytechnic School.
- Bill Gates is a college dropout.

YOU TOO CAN DO IT!

Plant a dream deep, water it daily, and do not let the weeds of doubt choke it, and your dreams will become a reality.

20

EXAM ANXIETY

My exams were near,
And I was full of fear,
I studied till late night,
So my answers would be right
I don't want to live for ever,
Because I know I am not clever
I wouldn't sleep a wink.
Just think, think and think,
If I don't pass,
I'd be in the same class!
The next day was creepy,
And I was sleepy
On the exam table,
I tried to be stable,
I was very shocked
To see the clock,
For I had slept
All through the exam.

– Shared by a student

Who develops "severe" examination fear?

a) A student who has failed in any previous examination

b) A student with low self-esteem

c) A student who has a lot of pressure from teachers/parents or even from himself

d) Someone who is appearing for a crucial examination

e) A student who has selected a few chapters and tries to read only those chapters

f) A student who is afraid of severe punishment or bad future for himself

Handling exam anxiety

- Identify the cause of anxiety.
- Fight negative thinking.
- Set a realistic goal.
- Follow same schedule.
- Eat and sleep well.
- Make a worry book.
- Talk to someone trustworthy.

How to reduce examination fear?

- Do not worry about the past failure. Learn a lesson from it. Analyse your past performance, make amends and take it as an experience.
- Follow correct study techniques.
- When the examination is nearing, do not study afresh, do only revision.
- If you still feel tensed up, do breathing exercises.
- Do not entertain doubts about your ability to do well in the examination.
- Do not anticipate failure or scoring less marks.

Day before the exam

- Plan ahead. Double-check the time and place of the exam and plan at what time you must leave home.

- Make sure you have everything you need to write with ready the day before.
- Do positive thinking. Avoid negative thoughts.
- Do not study late in the night. Have proper sleep.
- Talk to someone about your anxiety.

On the day of the exam

- Eat a good breakfast. Do not eat something which will leave a bad taste in the mouth or which leaves fibres stuck in the teeth.
- Take care of your digestive system, have proper bowel movement before you go to the exam.
- Tell yourself that you have done the best preparation.
- Check if you have taken everything required for the exam.
- Make up your mind not to get influenced negatively by what friends are talking. Remember you have done your "best preparation".

The great "hour" has arrived

- READ the paper word by word and understand it the way it is.
- Mark the questions which are the easiest.
- DO NOT get nervous if you find a question difficult to answer.
- Take deep breath and confidently start answering the question paper, beginning with the easy ones first.
- Write legibly.
- After you complete the paper, underline the important points.

- Check and recheck in case you have left out something, or if there are spelling mistakes, or if the correct question number is written against the relevant answer.
- At the end most people remember something they wish they had said or done. Reassure yourself that everyone feels like this and it is very rare for anyone to do a perfect exam. Even if you feel you did badly on the day, you cannot change what is past – but you will have lots more opportunities to do well in your lives.

I can't stop worrying that I might fail.

Your anxiety is understandable. At the same time it may have a harmful effect on you at this stage. Think truthfully and realistically. Have you ever failed before? If not then, why do you have this fear now? (Can you think of a specific reason?) If you have failed before, what were the causes of your failure at that time? Put it down in writing and discuss it with someone. Also think if the worst comes to the worst, what can happen? What will be the consequences? By realizing that the pressure is not half as bad as you imagine, you can stop fretting and clear your mind so that you can work peacefully.

Butterflies in your stomach?

Focus on your breathing, they will disappear and you would be able to calm yourself. Regular breathing introduces a meditative state of mind that helps you stay level-headed.

Take time to think

As you read the question paper, it is likely that students around you will already be starting to write. Let them do it and remind yourself to work at your own pace; **an early start and a high word count do not spell exam success.** You need time to read, understand and reflect. Do not hurry. Take your time.

My mom is more interested in other children's grades.

Planning for fun – after the exams

What are your plans after the exams? How do you plan to enjoy yourself?

Make a list of all the things you plan to do during vacation. How would you feel after the exams? Make specific plans after the exams. If you want to watch a movie, which movie? If you want to go out with friends, write where you would like to go. Every day spend five minutes planning seriously about your vacation. I am sure the thought itself makes you filled with joy.

There is nothing wrong in planning for your vacation. However, put in the same amount of sincerity while you are preparing for your crucial exam. If you have done well in the exam, your joy would double up.

I can understand how it feels Mom! I too hate these memos as much as you do.

DO IT NOW!

Do you have hard work to do? Do it *now*.

Do you have a kind word to say? Say it *now*.

If you have missed an opportunity in the past, it is not worth regretting,

And it is unwise waiting for a future moment to do anything,

For future cannot be trusted.

Now is the time to act.

Only *now* is yours,

Seize it and make full use of it.

If you have hard work to do, do it *now*.

Today the skies are clear and blue,

Tomorrow clouds may come in view,

Yesterday is not for you

Do it *now*.

21

A Rational Approach to Challenging Negative Thoughts

When people are very anxious, they tend to exaggerate how threatening a situation is, and to underplay how effectively they can cope with that situation. Our thoughts are distorted by our emotional state, and it can help to take a step back and evaluate the situation more realistically when you feel calm. Below is a rational approach to put the fears into a proper perspective, to challenge their validity, or to find an alternative view of your situation. Ask yourself questions such as these:

- Are you judging yourself harshly?
- Are you focusing on your failures and forgetting your successes?
- Have you managed to survive similar situations in the past (or even to succeed despite them)?
- Are you assuming that you know what will happen in the future?
- What evidence have you got that your fears are valid?
- Are you exaggerating the chance of something going wrong or minimizing the possibility of your working it out fine?
- Are you spending time frightening yourself about situations that you are not actually facing at present, and which may never happen?

- Are you comparing yourself to others?
- Are you assuming that everyone else is doing fine except you, when you do not actually know how others are feeling or managing?
- Are you blaming yourself for things that you cannot control, or are not your responsibility?

Two examples of challenging irrational thinking:

Irrational: "I'll make a fool of myself in front of all the classmates, and they would laugh at me."

Rational: "A lot of people will be feeling anxious like me. If I try to be confident and positive, I should be able to do it well. Last time I did not get any negative comment."

Irrational: "I am going to fail in my exams."

Rational: "I have been doing good revision. The work is supposed to be more challenging. I've done OK in the last test."

22

Time Management

Imagine you had a bank that credited you with Rs 86,400 every morning. You would have freedom to use as much of this money as you like. But there would be just one condition – at the end of the day, whatever balance is left will simply be taken away. What would you do in such a case? Obviously make full use of all the money.

Sadly, most of us do not realize that this is what we must do with time. Every day has 86,400 seconds that you can use as you like. Many students tend to waste most of the time they have for unimportant things. Use the following chart to see how you are using your time.

Use time effectively

To get a clear picture, please fill up accurately, and of course, honestly.

Formula: A multiplied by B = C

A	B	C
Number of hours per day	Number of days per week	Number of hours per week

Total all C and then deduct from 168 (number of hours per week).

That will be the time left for your study during a week.

	A	B	C
Avg. sleep including afternoon			
Avg. time spent in school/college			
Avg. commuting time			
Avg. grooming activities			
Avg. eating and relaxing			
Avg. newspaper reading time			
Avg. computer and TV time			
Avg. recreation time in a week (Including commuting time)			
Avg. extra tuition time in a week (Including commuting time)			
Avg. talking on phone			

Now that you are aware where your time is going, try to bring in the changes as per your needs. Analyse to find out which needs to be cut down.

23

Case Study

Do you recognize Sagar?

Sagar has revision work to do. He meant to start it weeks ago but has (typically) kept putting it off. His deadline is very close now, so he is quite anxious to get going.

He starts at 5 p.m. First it takes him half an hour to collect all his materials because he cannot remember where he put his notes. By the time all his equipment is ready – pens, paper, books and files neatly arranged – he feels very hungry. He goes to the kitchen and attacks the box of cookies. He opens his social studies book and realizes his notes are not complete. He calls up Amit and takes the notes on phone. By the time he is back to his study table it is...oh 6.45 p.m.!

"It is an odd time to start." So he waits for 7 p.m. Then he starts on page 1, line 1, of his notes. At 7:30 he casually flicks through his file and sees with horror that he has another 35 pages to go. As he calculates how long this will take, he escapes into a daydream that lasts ten precious minutes. At 7:45 he realizes he is wasting too much time and the guilt makes him feel worse, so he feels depressed. He cannot concentrate anymore.

What do you think Sagar should have done? Point out his mistakes.

List of Sagar's mistakes

1. ....

2. ....

3. ....

4. ....

5. ....

Do you make any of those mistakes?

THINGS WHICH YOU CANNOT GET BACK IN YOUR LIFE

Things which you cannot get back

Life which you have lost

Be careful about your health, attitude, lifestyles and live long.

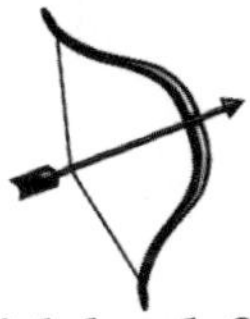

Arrow which has left the bow

Have clarity in the direction of your life.

An opportunity missed

Do not lose any opportunity in life.

Words spoken

Think twice before you speak.

Time that is wasted

Do not waste your time.

24

Get Organized

Any time of the year is a good time to make resolutions. If yours include getting better grades, you might want to start with getting organized. A few easy guidelines can help you to organize your schoolbooks, and you can use these tips to organize the rest of your life too!

- Make a schedule of your day: what time you go to school, what time you arrive home, how long it takes you to complete your homework, household chores (if any) and recreational activities. From there you can determine how much free time you have and schedule your day so that everything can be completed.
- Make a list of things you want to do. When you find yourself sitting and watching TV for hours or just doing nothing and being bored, use your list to change your time into productive time.
- Reduce the clutter. The less you have to organize, the quicker a process it will be. This means going through your exercise books and throwing out those which you do not need any longer; it could be old invitation cards or the page of doodles you scribbled while you were talking on the phone. Be careful not to throw out any important notes that you may want to refer to later. Having to reorganize yourself each day can waste much time.
- Set goals for what you want to accomplish. Make your goals specific. For example, "I want to score good marks"

is not a goal. "I want to score 10% more than my previous test" is a specific goal. It is much easier to reach a goal when you have something specific and realistic in mind.

- Divide your daily activities into categories and decide on the priority of each category. Completing homework is a priority. Getting exercise is a priority. Hanging out with friends is not. Set your activities based on their priority.
- Set time limits for yourself and then work to complete them within the time limits.
- Keep as much routine as possible in your day. Knowing what you need to do and when you need to do will help you to accomplish more.
- Do not procrastinate. Procrastination causes waste of time. (Refer to chapter 15 for tips)
- Take your time to complete a task correctly the first time itself. Having to redo your work all over again can waste time.
- Stack homework books, textbooks, and rough notebooks separately. Make sure you have enough space to spread your books on the table.
- Get all the important papers and file them together, so you can refer back to them whenever needed. If they were important enough to keep, they were too important to risk losing.
- Make sure each book is clearly labelled so you do not have to keep searching for a book each time.
- Have a small alarm clock on your table.
- Done all that? Great, now you can get on with organizing the rest of your life the same way. Reduce the clutter, separate everything by topic, label everything, and keep

a record of your progress. And **one more tip – do it today, the mess will be bigger by tomorrow.**

I've tried but cannot work with a timetable. What do I do?
Try having a daily time quota; be realistic while fixing the quota. Fix up how many hours of revision you will do per day. Make sure by the end of the week you have completed certain number of hours. You can reconsider your quota each week.

I am bored of solving the same problem for the third time, aren't you ?

25

Tips for Parents to Help Children Handle Exam Stress

Often children share with me, "Ma'am I knew everything . . . I had prepared so well but when I saw the question paper my mind went blank...." It is very common to hear this kind of a thing. Without exaggeration let me tell you this happens because of 'performance anxiety'. I have come across children who literally tremble when their exams are approaching for fear of "What if I don't do well?" They are frightened of the consequences. It is very important to give support to children.

Children who have experienced stress for some time need extra patience and reassurance. They might respond to a combination of the following:

Physical contact: Hugging helps children relax and builds self-esteem.

Listening: Ask children how they feel and **listen** to them. Spend time with your children to foster a healthy and supportive family relationship. It makes them feel secure.

Encouragement: Help children find something they are good at and tell them how proud you are of them.

Honesty and openness: Talk and encourage children to express their feelings openly. Be sensitive to children's feelings and let them know that you recognize that they have a problem.

Security: Try to be consistent in disciplining them. Bring as much order and consistency in children's life as possible. Reassure them that all kids have pressures and fears and they are not alone.

Physical exercise: Exercise helps burn off stressful feelings.

Humour: Help children see the funny side of things.

Quiet: Allow for quiet time.

Balanced diet: Encourage children to eat a healthy, varied diet.

Teach children to recognize the symptoms of stress and the changes they feel in themselves – e.g. rapid heartbeat, sweaty palms, fast breathing, headaches, tummy aches, tight tense muscles and nervous panicky feelings. Find out about any significant events in the children's lives. Caring adults are very important for children. Provide an environment that promotes a relaxed lifestyle. When adults observe the behaviour of children closely, they soon become skilled at determining when they are under stress.

More than the academic excellence, it is the self-esteem and self-confidence of a child that brings him success. Your trust in him will make him feel reassured and calmer.

Ideal revision guide

Revise the day after learning something (when it is still fresh in your mind). Revise it again a week later.

One month after that second revision, revise for a third time. A fourth and final revision after a term should ensure that the information stays permanently in your mind.

How can teachers be so cruel? Who is responsible if my mom faints seeing this report card?

I don't know how to cope with my teacher. I find it impossible to please her.
I would say you are luckier than others. The teacher might have seen potential in you. That is why she/he has expectations. Try not to think of pleasing her; instead try finding a higher purpose in your learning. It will not be a burden when you do something for your own sake – not for anyone else's sake.

26

SQ3RT – The Essence of Study Techniques

If you ask me, "how to study effectively?" and tell me to answer in just one word, I will say SQ3RT! This is a time-tested technique. Mastering this technique will help you increase your grasping power dramatically. SQ3RT consists of the following steps:

Survey: First survey the chapter, the title, the heading and subheadings, captions under picture, charts, graphs or maps. This will help your mind to get in frame for absorbing information and create a good background.

Question: While you are surveying, turn the title, heading or subheading into a question. Read the question at the end of the chapter and ask yourself, "What do I know about this subject?" Also ask a question about what you think is important.

Read: After you have asked the questions, set out on the reading mission. **Read with full understanding**, answer the question at the end of the chapters and note all the underlined, italicized, bold-printed words. Read captions under pictures, graphics, etc. Reduce your speed for difficult passages. Stop and reread parts which are not clear. Take notes while reading.

Recite: After you have read a section, orally ask yourself questions about what you have just read. Take notes from the text but write the information in your own words. Underline/ highlight important points you have just read. Once you have read something you need to speak out loudly the points that you have learned. What will happen then is that you will also hear the material, giving a double effect.

Review/Revise: It is an ongoing process. Refine your mental organization and begin building memory. Once you have finished the entire chapter using the preceding steps, go back over all the questions from all the headings. See if you can still answer them. If not, look back and refresh your memory, then continue. The review can be done in small chunks of time as you wait between classes, or have some time to spare while waiting for friends or between classes or during lunch. Engaging in short periods of intensive concentration is a very efficient study method.

Test: After a gap of a few days, test yourself on whatever you have learnt. Testing is one of the most important points because if you are not able to recollect something, you have a chance to learn it again. If you do not test, you may remain under the false impression that you know it very well.

> *No shortcuts to hard work. Everything must be followed as routine, which later becomes a habit.*

My mind is as blank as the blackboard...
could you help me Miss?

27

Value Yourself

Value yourself

A well-known speaker started off his seminar by holding up a $500 note. In the room of 200, he asked, "Who would like this note?" Hands started going up. He said, "I am going to give this note to one of you, but first let me do this." He proceeded to crumple the note up. He then asked, "Who still wants it?" still the hands were up in the air. "Well!" he replied, "What if I do this?" and he dropped it on the ground and started to grind it into the floor with the shoe. He picked it up, now all crumpled and dirty. "Now who still wants it?" still the hands went into the air.

Value has a value only if its value is valued by you.

"My friends, you have all learned a very valuable lesson. No matter what I did to the money, you still wanted it because it did not decrease in value. It was still worth $500. **Many times in our lives, we are dropped, crumpled and ground into the dirt by the decisions we make and the circumstances that come our way. We feel as though we are worthless. But no matter what has happened or what will happen, you will never lose your value. You are special; do not ever forget it!** Never let yesterday's disappointments overshadow tomorrow's dream."

28

ABOUT ANGER

Dear Student

Many children come to me asking for tips to "control" their anger. "Controlling" never helps. You must learn to **manage** anger. Anger is a very normal and natural emotion in every human being. It is important to realize that everyone gets angry. However, the way we handle anger can be different. People use a variety of both conscious and unconscious processes to deal with their angry feelings. Some people are destructive when they get angry. Some people verbalize their anger. Some people internalize their angry feelings. They are unable to properly express their anger verbally or physically. It is not wise to put off dealing with anger. One must find constructive ways of dealing with anger.

If the same "mean" thing happened to ten people, they all would react differently. Some of the ten people would get mad, some would get afraid, some would feel sad, and some would blow off. What makes the difference? Why do different people react differently to the same event? The difference is the personal history of the person and how they have learned to deal with threat, stresses or losses. As the early philosophers said, "it is not what happens to you, but how you deal with it that counts."

There are different things we can do with our ANGER

- We can use anger to lash out at others and intimidate them.
- We can turn it inward and beat ourselves up.
- We can use it to speak out with firmness and increase our self-esteem.
- We can use it to correct a situation that is wrong.

What do *you* do with your anger?

Facts about anger

- Everyone gets angry. This is normal.
- You cannot control the people or situations that make you angry. You CAN control what you do with anger.
- Handling anger in a negative way leads to negative consequences leading to a negative reputation leading to a poor self-image.
- When you are angry (a) remain calm (b) stop and think about what you should do and what will happen when you do it (c) if you lose control and handle your anger in a negative way, figure out what you did wrong so that you can learn from your mistakes.
- Know your signals that tell you are getting angry. This way you can prevent yourself from losing control.
- Do not allow anger to control you. You have the power to control your anger.

Some people verbalize their anger, whereas others internalize their feelings. Expressing your angry feelings in an assertive – **not aggressive** – manner is the healthiest way to express anger.

Strategies to deal with anger

- Get away from the situation/person.
- Take deep breaths. Inhale. Exhale slowly.
- Do some exercises or go for a brisk walk.
- Count up to ten or till you feel angry feelings settling down.
- Take a hot bath or a cold shower.
- Lie down and relax with your legs raised.
- Drink a glass of cold water.
- Write your feelings.
- Phone a friend.

About anger

There is only one person on the face of this earth

Who has the power to make you angry.

That person is YOURSELF!

And likewise, you are the only person who can create peace of mind!

It is OK to feel angry.

It is not OK to hurt yourself or others with your anger.

Increase your self-esteem by expressing your anger in safe and healthy ways.

Understand your anger and use it in ways that are helpful to you and others.

You don't have to hold onto your anger.

You can learn to let it go.

Change your angry thoughts and you change your life!

What is one of the biggest dangers on earth?
Take out the letter 'D' from Danger, i.e. Anger.
Anger is harmful to you and others. Learn to manage it.

The best way to deal with anger is to talk about it. Express your angry feelings to someone who can understand it, may be a counsellor or a close adult family member.

> *Anyone can become angry – that is easy. But to be angry at the right person, to the right degree, at the right time, for the right purpose, and in the right way – that is not easy.*
>
> —Aristotle

29

Parents' Guide to Encouraging a Child

We enjoy doing things that we like. But when we perceive tasks as difficult, inconvenient or scary, we may shift into our procrastination mode. We have very clear ways of fooling ourselves by giving excuses like "I'll wait until I am in the mood to do it," or "I've got too many other things to do it first," or "It's too hard to talk about. I do not know where to begin." Children too do the same thing, so the first and foremost thing is to be calm when the child does it. Take note of a few things before you react.

Analyse rationally: First try to find out the reason why he is doing so. Is he finding it boring/difficult; and how can you help him? Does he need extra help for a particular subject? Is he able to understand what is being taught at school?

Do not make rash judgements: Jumping to the conclusion that he will fail or that he is no good at that subject will only create a wall of fear. Instead, focus on what positive steps you can take towards helping him. Do sit with him and test him for effective learning. Make up questions on the information gained and have him answer emphasizing on the important points.

Design clear goals: Think about what the child's need is and what practical remedy can be used. Be specific. Keep your sights within reason. Having goals too big can scare the child more. Preferably, construct a schedule for the child with his help. The schedule could be on a weekly basis, e.g. doing 3 lessons of English and 3 lessons of science by Saturday or finishing last year's test papers of two subjects by Tuesday. The schedule could change as monotony sets in. You can even sit with the child and make a new schedule for every week or two weeks. Sunday evening may be the most convenient time to do this.

Break the goals into sub-goals: Once goals are set, break them into subgoals. For example, if the child is to finish test papers of English and maths by Tuesday, then Monday morning 6:30–7:30 practise maths, evening 5–6 preview English and prepare for the test. Review again on Tuesday morning and test on Tuesday 5–6 p.m. It is always better to inform the child well in advance to enable him to get organized.

Help the child get organized: Help him get the material ready before he begins. This must be done on a regular basis. Seeing whether his class work is complete or not, if all the textbooks and notebooks are kept in order or not. Consistency is a must. Firing him one day for being disorganized and then not supervising for months together will not fetch results.

Reward the child: VERY IMPORTANT. Pat the child, acknowledge when he has achieved a goal or a subgoal. It will motivate him to follow further schedules. Do not minimize the accomplishments even if it looks like that to you. Let him watch his favourite serial on TV or take him out on a drive on weekend.

Study environment analysis: Identify the right place for the child to study, which is away from distractions like phone, computer or TV, or music system. The place should be away from visitors or people talking. For small children there should be no toys around, and for a little older ones no storybooks should be in sight. Study table must have only school textbooks and notebooks.

Leave some unscheduled time for flexibility: This is very important! Lack of flexibility could be the reason for the schedule to fail. Sometimes children overshoot their time, for that particular subject, flexibility will help them get back without upsetting the schedule much.

Allot time for recreation: Recreation is a must for refreshing the mind. If the child has got scheduled recreational activities, take them into account while planning. In case the child does not have scheduled time, you fix up a time for recreational activities or simply playing. Do not cut down on that. Grounding the child (especially during exam time), stopping all activities will not help.

Where does time go? "There is very little time and so much to study." This is a common statement. It may seem like there are not enough hours in the week to get everything done, especially for children of higher standards.That may be true or it may be that the child is not using his time as efficiently as possible. To assess where the time goes, help the child do a small test (based on the sample given on page 61).

Relieve stress: Most important of all is the point that you must see to it that the child is relieved of any kind of stress. The child himself may be tensed up about his studies, try to help him work out things for himself, instead of adding to his worries. Keep him away from any emotional disturbance as far as possible.

The last word...

- ***Please*** *balance expectations and motivations. Even if a child is performing well, he will have anxiety whether he will live up to the expectation of his teachers and parents. Remember that the* ***education system is not a barometer of abilities, and every child cannot be good in every subject.***
- ***Provide*** *silent emotional support.*
- ***Never*** *compare.*
- ***It is proven fact*** *that good self-esteem is more important than academic excellence for his success in life.*
- *Make sure they eat well, sleep well, get enough exercise and LAUGH a lot.*

Fear sees obstacles. Faith sees opportunities.

Fear sees problems. Faith sees possibilities.

Fear sees stumbling blocks. Faith sees stepping stones.

Points to ponder

Date..............................Day.............................Time.....................

Moments which made an impression today

Today the day turned out to be ....

Because ....

Today I want to thank

....

For ....

Today I would like to say sorry ....

Because ....

Today I would like to blame...

For

....

Today I envied ....

....

A good deed I did today ....

I am proud of myself today because ....

I am angry with myself today because...................................

Help Yourself

No one knows you better than yourself.

No one knows what is in your mind.

No one knows what is happening to you.

No one can think for you.

No one can feel for you.

No one can force you to do anything.

No one but YOU can help yourself.

Notes

Notes

Notes

Notes